Beautiful Summer

An Adult Coloring Book

For Any Question and Suggestions
robberfickle@gmail.com

This Book Belongs To

....

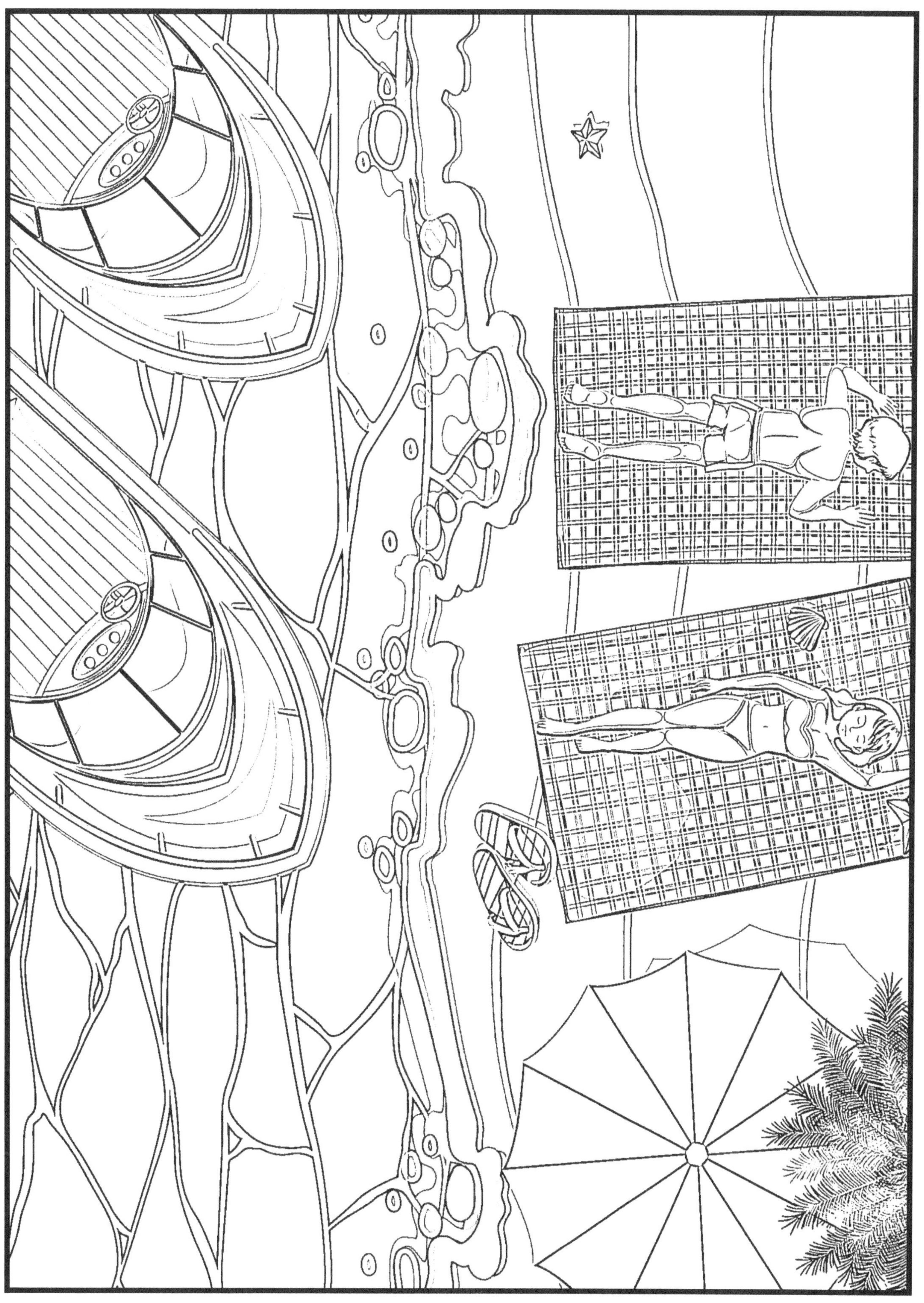

Life's a Beach!

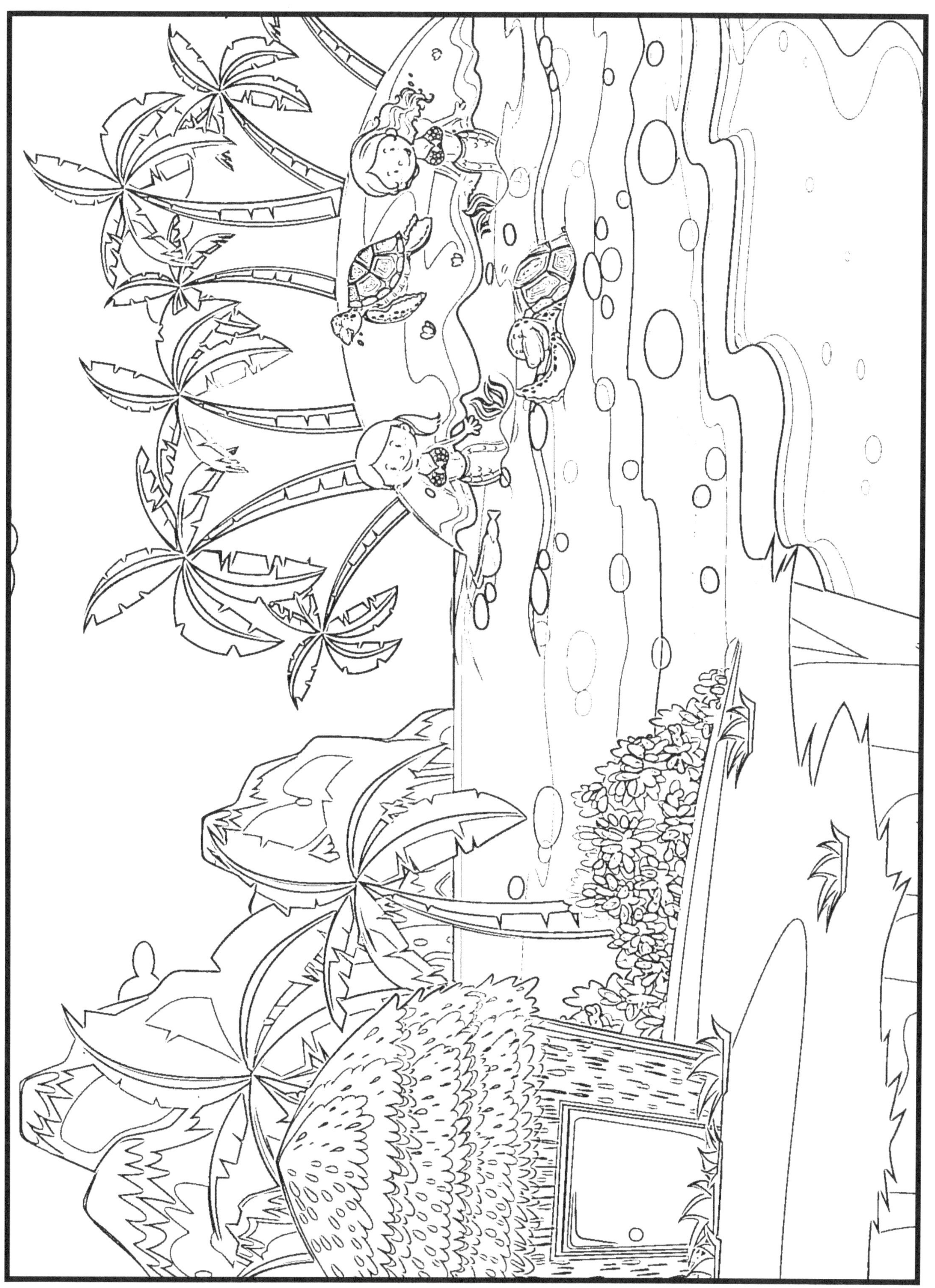

www.ingramcontent.com/pod-product-compliance
Lightning Source LLC
Chambersburg PA
CBHW081633250726
48657CB00009B/2865